THE AUDUBON SOCIETY POCKET GUIDES

A Chanticleer Press Edition

John L. Behler, Curator of Herpetology
New York Zoological Society

FAMILIAR REPTILES AND AMPHIBIANS

Alfred A. Knopf, New York

This is a Borzoi Book
Published by Alfred A. Knopf, Inc.

Prepared and produced by Chanticleer Press, Inc.,
New York.
Color reproductions by Reprocolor International s.r.l.,
Milan, Italy.
Typeset by Dix Type Inc., Syracuse, New York.
Printed and bound by Dai Nippon, Tokyo, Japan.

First Printing.

Library of Congress Catalog Number: 87-46098
ISBN: 0-394-75793-9

Contents

Introduction

The Reptiles and Amphibians

Appendices

How to Use This Guide　　　Watching reptiles and amphibians is a rewarding pastime that will add much to your enjoyment of any trip outdoors. These creatures are common everywhere, and learning to find and identify them is fun and challenging, whether you are in your own backyard, a city park, or a nature preserve.

Coverage　　This guide fully covers 80 of the most common and distinctive reptiles and amphibians in North America, from the Arctic to the Mexican border and from the Atlantic Coast to the Pacific. An additional 80 species are included under the heading "Similar Species," raising to 160 the total number of reptiles and amphibians described in this guide.

Organization　　This easy-to-use pocket guide is divided into three parts: introductory essays; illustrated accounts of the reptiles and amphibians; and appendices.

Introduction　　Two introductory essays will help you to use and enjoy the guide. "Identifying Reptiles and Amphibians" tells you what to look for and suggests questions to ask yourself when you see an unfamiliar reptile or amphibian. "Finding Reptiles and Amphibians" gives practical clues about where and when to go and what to do in order to discover

6

these often secretive animals. Black-and-white drawings show the important parts of reptiles and amphibians.

The Reptiles and Amphibians
This section includes 80 color plates, arranged visually by shape, color, and overall appearance. Major groups of North American reptiles and amphibians are represented. Facing each color plate is a description of the important field marks of the species, as well as notes on other species with which it might be confused, and descriptions of its habitat and range. For quick reference, a map showing each species' distribution supplements the range statement. An introductory paragraph provides interesting facts about each species' habits, history, or close relatives. The symbol ⬡ indicates venomous reptiles.

Appendices
Following the species accounts, a special section "Guide to Orders and Families" describes the major orders and families covered in this book. Remembering the distinguishing features of these broad categories will help you to identify a species more quickly and easily.

Wherever you live, there are colorful and interesting reptiles and amphibians to see and enjoy. The more you know about them the more you will appreciate them and understand the natural world.

Identifying Reptiles and Amphibians

Almost everyone knows a frog, a turtle, and a snake—they are distinctive animals that are easily recognized by their shapes. But telling different amphibians and reptiles from one another is often difficult, because they share similar forms and coloring. Look for important features, such as shape, behavior, size, range and habitat, color and pattern, and voice.

Shape
An experienced observer analyzes amphibian and reptile shapes carefully. To the untrained eye, all snakes may look alike. But look more closely. Is the snake streamlined or stout, long-tailed or short? Does it have round or vertical pupils? Look at the head. Is it lance-shaped? Is there a deep pit between the eye and nostril? Use the same sorts of distinguishing features to identify frogs, salamanders, turtles, and lizards.

Behavior
Notice the animal's habitat and observe its position, actions, and the time of activity. Is it nocturnal, diurnal, or active at twilight? How does it move?

Size
Amphibians and reptiles continue to grow during life. The sizes offered here are total length ranges for adults. Without holding the animal, it is difficult to judge size. However, if you learn the sizes of common species in your

8

area, you can easily compare them against your size impressions of an unfamiliar one.

Range and Habitat Unlike birds, amphibians and reptiles—with rare exceptions—do not travel far. Thus, where an animal is found is an important clue to its identification. The maps and range descriptions give basic distributions. Within a range amphibians and reptiles have specific habitat requirements. Learning both range and habitat will help you narrow down the possibilities so you can identify your species.

Color and Pattern Identification based upon colors and patterns is difficult. Markings vary with age, sex, or locality, and often differ greatly even among related offspring. And colors, especially in frogs and some lizards, may change in minutes. Don't rely on color alone to identify your species.

Voice Male frogs and toads have distinctive breeding calls which can be helpful in identification. Compare the sounds you hear with descriptions in the text, and check that the habitat and time of year are correct.

Types of Amphibians

Costal groove

Salamander

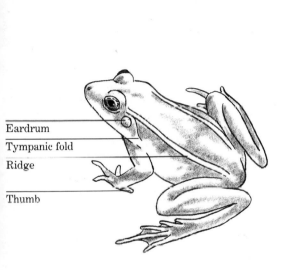

Eardrum

Tympanic fold

Ridge

Thumb

Parotoid gland

Warts

Frog

Toad

Types of Reptiles

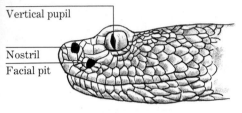

Vertical pupil

Nostril

Facial pit

Pit Viper

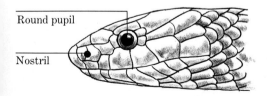

Round pupil

Nostril

Harmless Snake

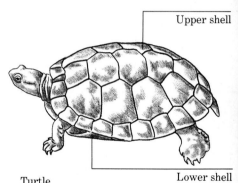

Upper shell

Lower shell

Turtle

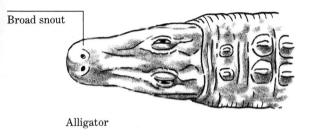

Broad snout

Alligator

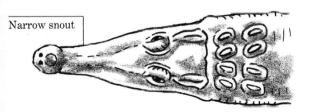

Narrow snout

Crocodile

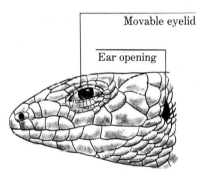

Movable eyelid

Ear opening

Lizard

Finding Reptiles and Amphibians

In most areas, salamanders, frogs, turtles, lizards, and snakes are considerably more common than most people believe. Observing them requires patience, but if you know their activities and habitats, you'll quickly become proficient at spotting these elusive animals and locating their retreats.

Season and Time

The time of year and the time of day are very important when planning an outing. Except for the breeding season—when salamanders leave their secret retreats for mating sites and male frogs and toads call to prospective mates—amphibians are rarely seen or heard. Many amphibians are nocturnal and are encountered in numbers only during late winter or spring rains. But with some species, breeding coincides with summer or autumn downpours.

The conditions amphibians prefer are often too cool for reptile activity. In temperate areas, reptiles are inactive from October or November to March or April. In the Deep South, they may be active nearly year-round. In summer, most reptiles shun midday heat and appear only in the morning or late afternoon, and some become nocturnal. The opposite behavior occurs during the cooler periods of their active season.

Where to Look   Learning where amphibians and reptiles live is an important first step to successfully observing them. Amphibians rarely wander far from a source of moisture: wet meadows, the sides of stream courses, ponds, lakes, spring seepages, and swamps are all home to salamanders and frogs. Reptiles are found in these habitats too, but they also exploit drier environments—open wooded hillsides, sandhill country, prairies, and desert scrub—because their scaly skin protects them from losing water. Be sure also to look under flat rocks, pieces of bark, logs, leaf litter, or in stump holes or tunnels—favorite retreats for both amphibians and reptiles. Piles of construction debris as well as abandoned farm buildings and their attendant rubble are ideal reptile hiding places.

Rural Roads   On rainy nights during the breeding season, scores of frogs and salamanders may be seen along little-traveled roads that pass near temporary ponds or flooded ditches. Reptiles may also appear near roads when temperatures exceed 65°F. The best roads are heat-retaining rural blacktops and dirt roads that pass through wetlands or undisturbed habitats. A four-hour period beginning about an hour before dusk—just after an afternoon shower or during an evening rain—is the ideal time.

THE REPTILES AND AMPHIBIANS

Bullfrog *Rana catesbeiana*

North America's largest frog species, the Bullfrog is usually the last to begin calling its deep, resonant *jug-o-rum* or *brr-uum* in summer. Females may lay up to 20,000 eggs; tadpoles take almost two years to transform and two to three more years to mature. Bullfrogs have voracious appetites, and large ones have been known to consume small birds and young snakes. Males are territorial; a rival entering the turf of a calling male risks a wrestling match.

Identification 3½–8″. Back yellowish-green to brown, sometimes mottled with dark brown. Large external eardrum and well-developed tympanic folds. No ridge at juncture of back and sides.

Similar Species Pig Frog (*R. grylio*), 3–6¼″, has a pointed snout, and its longest toe is webbed nearly to tip; SE. Coastal Plain. Green Frog has prominent ridges.

Habitat Large ponds, lakes, and slow streams with vegetation.

Range SE. Wyoming to Nova Scotia south to Texas and Florida; introduced from British Columbia to S. California.

18

Green Frog *Rana clamitans*

During summer, adults are usually found at or close to the water's edge; the young may venture into wet fields or marshlands to forage. Green Frogs breed from May well into the summer months. Their call note sounds like the twang of a banjo string. Males are territorial and defend a portion of their shoreline against rivals; they issue a warning call to intruders.

Identification 2–4″. Color highly variable; may be green, bronze, or brown. Large external eardrum; prominent ridges extend from sides to middle of back.

Similar Species Mink Frog (*R. septentrionalis*), 1¾–3″, has a strong, musky odor, absent or weakly developed ridge at juncture of back and sides, and bright green, unmarked lips; SE. Manitoba and Minnesota to Labrador, south to N. New York. Bullfrog lacks ridges.

Habitat Shallow water; springs, swamps, creeks, and edges of lakes and ponds.

Range S. Ontario to Nova Scotia, south to E. Texas and N. Florida.

Northern Cricket Frog *Acris crepitans*

Lacking enlarged toe pads, cricket frogs are nonclimbing members of the treefrog family. When startled, they move away with quick, erratic, yard-long leaps. Their cricketlike call, resembling the sound of smooth pebbles being clicked together in rapid succession, may be heard day and night from April through July. Cricket frogs are cold-hardy and are active year-round in the Deep South.

Identification ⅝–1½". Dark triangle between eyes and dark ragged stripe along thigh; skin warty, highly variable in color. Snout rounded; hind feet extensively webbed.

Similar Species Southern Cricket Frog (*A. gryllus*), ⅝–1¼", has pointed snout and clean-cut stripe on thigh; SE. Coastal Plain. Northern Chorus Frog has white stripe along upper lip; lacks thigh stripe.

Habitat Sunny riverside marshes, open mudflats, and sparsely vegetated shoreline of ponds, lakes, and streams.

Range Nebraska east to Long Island and south to Texas and the Florida panhandle.

Northern Leopard Frog *Rana pipiens*

Great wanderers, leopard frogs may move as much as a mile away from water during the summer into moist fields, meadows, and pastures. Early breeders, they migrate to breeding ponds from the larger waters where they hibernate, arriving at the time Wood Frogs are finishing reproduction. The male's call is a low, rattling snore interspersed with clucking notes.

Identification 2–5″. Streamlined; brown or green with 2 or 3 rows of large, irregularly spaced, cream-bordered chocolate spots between prominent ridges at juncture of back and sides. Light stripe on upper jaw. Belly white.

Similar Species Southern Leopard Frog (*R. sphenocephala*), 2–5″, has light spot on eardrum; SE. Kansas to Long Island, south to E. Texas and Florida Keys. Pickerel Frog has bright yellow groin and square blotches.

Habitat Wet meadows, floodplains of streams and rivers, weedy lake shallows, prairie potholes, springs, and bogs.

Range Fort Smith, Northwest Territories, and Labrador south to Arizona, Nebraska, Kentucky and S. New England.

24

Pickerel Frog *Rana palustris*

Unlike the leopard frogs, with which it is often confused, the Pickerel Frog does not venture far from water. If startled, it dives to the bottom. Its skin secretions make this frog distasteful or noxious to most potential predators and may kill other frogs placed in the same container or terrarium. The Pickerel Frog breeds during late winter and early spring, with the advent of heavy rains. Its mating call is a low-pitched croaking that sounds like snoring.

Identification 1¾–3¼". Slender and smooth-skinned, with 2 rows of square chocolate-brown blotches running down back between light-colored ridges at juncture of back and sides. Inner surface of thighs and groin golden yellow.

Similar Species Northern Leopard Frog lacks yellow groin.

Habitat Clear upland streams, bogs, spring seeps, lakes, and damp meadows; prefers areas with low, dense vegetation and cool waters.

Range Wisconsin east to Nova Scotia and south to E. Texas and N. Georgia.

26

Green Treefrog *Hyla cinerea*

From a distance the calls of these "rain frogs" sound like cowbells; closer, the sound is *quonk, quonk*. Green Treefrogs are especially active on damp or rainy evenings and are often attracted to lighted windows where insects have gathered. During the day, they rest motionless on vegetation. When frightened, they make gangly leaps into space.

Identification 1¼–2½". Long-legged and slender, with smooth, bright green or yellowish-green skin. Sharply defined light stripe along upper jaw and side; side stripe may be absent.

Similar Species Squirrel Treefrog (*H. squirella*), 1–1½", is green to brown, without distinct markings; SE. Coastal Plain. Barking Treefrog (*H. gratiosa*), 2–2¾", is plump with granular, dark-spotted skin; SE. Coastal Plain.

Habitat Lakes, ponds, streams, and swamps with abundant emergent vegetation.

Range S. Illinois south to E. Texas, and Delaware south along Coastal Plain to Florida Keys and west to S. Texas.

28

Pacific Treefrog *Hyla regilla*

This frog is the one most commonly heard along the Pacific Coast. When Hollywood movie directors require authentic nighttime sounds, the Pacific Treefrog obliges with its high-pitched, two-part *kreck-ek* call, uttered in rapid sequence. Contrary to its name, the Pacific Treefrog is often found on or near the ground in damp retreats among rocks, thick vegetation, or in animal burrows. It breeds from November to July.

Identification	¾–2″. Skin rough; color varies from green to light tan to black, often with dark spots on back and legs. Black stripe through eye; often has dark triangle between eyes. Large toe pads. Male has gray throat.
Similar Species	California Treefrog (*H. cadaverina*), 1–2″, lacks eye stripe; S. California.
Habitat	Amid low vegetation in a variety of habitats—drainage ditches, spring seeps, temporary ponds, reservoirs, streams, marshlands; sea level to over 11,000′.
Range	S. British Columbia east to W. Montana and south to Baja California.

30

Wood Frog *Rana sylvatica*

The Wood Frog is the only North American frog found north of the Arctic Circle. It often begins its reproductive activities before ponds are free of ice. Characterized as an explosive breeder, it may complete annual egg-laying within two to six days. Vocalizing males make short, raspy, ducklike quacks. In summer, Wood Frogs stray some distance from water.

Identification 1½–3¼". Dark "robber's mask" bordered by white stripe on upper jaw, both ending just behind eardrum. Prominent ridges at juncture of back and sides. Western representatives typically have light line down middle of back.

Similar Species Red-legged Frog has less distinct mask, is red below, and lacks back stripe.

Habitat Moist woodlands in East, grasslands and adjacent aspen thickets in Northwest, and tundra in Far North.

Range Alaska to Labrador, south through Appalachians to N. Georgia and N. South Carolina.

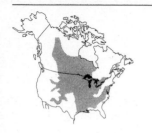

Northern Chorus Frog *Pseudacris triseriata*

Often heard but seldom seen, chorus frogs begin to call in winter in southern areas and with the first warm rains of spring northward. Their short, rasping trill has been likened to the sound made by running a fingernail over the teeth of a comb. Chorus frogs are exceptionally wary.

Identification ¾–1½". Small treefrog lacking toe pads. Dark stripe from snout through eye to groin; white stripe along upper lip; 3 dark stripes or series of longitudinal spots on back.

Similar Species Spotted Chorus Frog (*P. clarki*), ¾–1¼", has green blotches rimmed in black; Nebraska to Mexico. Southern Chorus Frog (*P. nigrita*), ¾–1¼", has 3 rows of black spots; SE. Coastal Plain. Cricket frogs (*Acris* species) have dark stripe on rear of thigh.

Habitat From prairies and marshes to moist woodlands, farmlands, and suburbia.

Range Northwest Territories east to New Jersey and south to Arizona, E. Texas, and North Carolina.

34

Gray Treefrog *Hyla versicolor*

Two species known as Gray Treefrogs (*H. chrysoscelis* and *H. versicolor*) are identical looking with ranges that overlap extensively. Scientists separate them by counting chromosomes and by their calls (*H. chrysoscelis* trills faster). Both of these treefrogs are superb climbers and may ascend high into trees to forage or to take refuge in knotholes.

Identification 1¼–2½″. Skin warty, typically gray, but may vary from pale brown to green with several dark blotches on back. Prominent light spot beneath eye. Undersurfaces of thighs bright orange or yellow. Large toe pads.

Similar Species Bird-voiced Treefrog (*H. avivoca*), 1–2″, is pale green to greenish-yellow on hidden surface of thigh; S. Illinois to Louisiana and Florida panhandle.

Habitat Margins of temporary pools, semipermanent ponds, flooded ditches, and surrounding woodlands.

Range S. Manitoba east to New Brunswick and south to E. Texas and N. Florida.

Red-legged Frog *Rana aurora*

The Red-legged is our largest native western frog. Surprisingly, its voice is weak, and the guttural, one-pitch series of its call can be heard only a short distance from the call site. As in other species of the true frog family, the male's forelimbs and thumbs become enlarged during the breeding season—January to March. In areas where the Bullfrogs live, the Red-legged Frog has declined in numbers or vanished.

Identification 2–5¼". Underside yellow, with red on lower abdomen; black and red mottling around groin. Dark mask bordered by light jaw stripe that ends in front of shoulder. Ridges at juncture of back and sides well developed. Back stippled with black flecks and blotches.

Similar Species Spotted Frog (*R. pretiosa*), 1¾–4", has jaw stripe that runs to shoulder, eyes upturned; SE. Alaska to Nevada.

Habitat Lowlands and foothills near marshes, ponds, lakes, and streams, and adjacent damp woods and meadows.

Range West of Cascade-Sierra ranges from SW. British Columbia to NW. Baja California.

Spring Peeper *Hyla crucifer*

Although extraordinarily common, peepers are seldom seen except during the breeding season when they cross roads during the first rains (March to July in Canada; March to April in the northern United States; and November to March in the southern United States). Their high-pitched, birdlike *pee-eeep* is among the earliest signs of spring; the collective voices sound like sleigh bells. After egg-laying, Spring Peepers forage for small invertebrates in nearby thickets.

Identification   ¾–1½". Small treefrog; tan, gray, or dark brown, with large dark X on back and dark bar between eyes. Males have dark throats and are smaller than females.

Similar Species   Pine Woods Treefrog (*H. femoralis*), 1–1¾", has yellow or orange spots on dark rear surface of thigh; SE. Coastal Plain.

Habitat   Temporary and permanent ponds in second-growth woodlands; swamps, bogs, marshes, drainage ditches.

Range   Manitoba to Nova Scotia, south to E. Texas and central Florida.

40

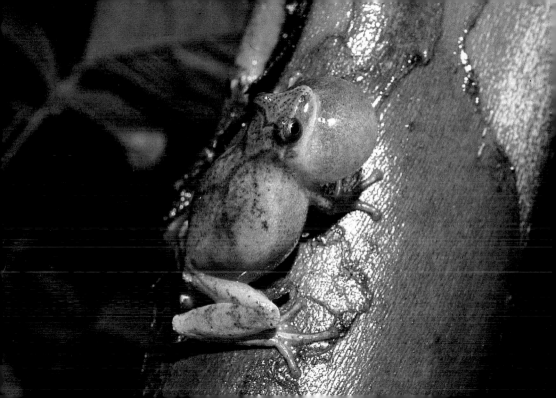

Eastern Spadefoot *Scaphiopus holbrooki*

The Eastern is the only spadefoot toad in the East; five others occur west of the Mississippi. All are nocturnal and adept at burrowing, using their spadelike hind feet to push soil aside as they back into the ground. Spadefoots are explosive breeders; a heavy rain may bring large numbers to the surface to take advantage of temporary breeding pools. An egg can develop into a tadpole and then into a toadlet in only two weeks.

Identification 1¾–3″. Black sickle-shaped spade on each hind foot. Eyes catlike; 2 yellowish lines beginning at eyes run down back to form lyre-shaped marking.

Similar Species Couch's Spadefoot (*S. couchi*), 2¼–3½″, has back yellowish or greenish with dark marbling. SE. California east to central Texas.

Habitat Dry sandy and loamy regions; open woodlands, pine barrens, floodplains of large rivers.

Range SE. Missouri to S. New England, south to E. Louisiana and Florida Keys; also E. Oklahoma and W. Arkansas south through E. Texas and W. Louisiana.

42

American Toad *Bufo americanus*

The familiar eastern "hop toad" is most active from twilight through the evening. Its mating call is a long musical trill that lasts 10 to 30 seconds. Breeding from January (in the South) to July (in the Far North); each female lays up to 12,000 eggs in long, twisting strings. Tadpoles metamorphose in five to ten weeks.

Identification 2–4⅜". Skin warty, usually brown but highly variable, nearly plain or with dark spotting with 1 or 2 warts per spot. Prominent kidney-shaped parotoid gland does not touch bony ridges on head except by short spur. Male has dark throat.

Similar Species Southern Toad (*B. terrestris*), 1⅝–4½", has conspicuously high bony ridges on head with knoblike swellings; SE. Coastal Plain. Common Toad has bony ridges that directly touch parotoid glands.

Habitat Near shallow water, from city parks and suburban gardens to marshlands and forested mountains.

Range SE. Manitoba to Labrador south to E. Oklahoma and Georgia.

44

Common Toad *Bufo woodhousei*

This is the toad most often seen at night catching insects attracted to lights. It breeds from March to July, appearing later in the season than the American Toad but before the Southern Toad (*B. terrestris*). Females lay up to 8,000 eggs; tadpoles transform in one to two months. The male's *w-a-a-a-ah* sounds like a sheep's bleat and lasts about one to four seconds.

Identification 2–5". Large; brown, green, or gray, with light stripe down center of back. Prominent bony ridges on head touch elongate parotoid glands.

Similar Species Western Toad (*B. boreas*), 2½–5", lacks bony ridges on head; Pacific Coast to Rockies and S. Alaska to N. Baja California. American Toad has bony ridges that do not touch parotoid glands except by short spur.

Habitat A variety of sandy or loamy habitats, from suburbia to coastal beaches and grasslands to wooded lowlands, along desert streams and into mountain canyons.

Range SE. Washington to S. New England; south to Florida panhandle and SE. California into Mexico.

46

Great Plains Toad *Bufo cognatus*

Large numbers of Great Plains Toads may congregate after a downpour in rain pools, drainage ditches, and flooded fields. Breeding takes place after a spring or summer storm. Females lay strings of as many as 20,000 eggs, and metamorphosis occurs in six to seven weeks. Calling males produce a harsh vibrating trill that lasts 10 to 15 seconds; when inflated, their vocal sacs are sausage-shaped and extend upward in front of their heads.

Identification 2–4½". Only North American toad with large, dark, light-bordered blotches in pairs on back. Bony ridges on head converge to form bony hump on snout. Color variable.

Similar Species Texas Toad (*B. speciosus*), 2–3½", has faint, if any, spots, weak or no bony ridges on head, and no stripe on back; S. New Mexico and SW. Kansas south to Texas.

Habitat Primarily grasslands and desert scrub.

Range Great Plains from SE. Alberta east to W. Minnesota and south into Mexico; W. Texas to extreme SE. California and south-central Utah.

48

Stinkpot *Sternotherus odoratus*

Stinkpots are poor swimmers, yet they are highly aquatic and adeptly exploit the bottom of weedy shallows for snails, insects, and crayfish. They bask on mats of vegetation or occasionally on tree limbs above the water. When disturbed, these feisty little musk turtles emit a foul-smelling fluid and bite.

Identification 3–5½". Tiny, with large head and pointed snout. Two light stripes accent face; 2 pairs of barbels on chin and throat. Upper shell smooth or keeled, olive-brown to dark gray, and often masked by algae. Lower shell small, with 11 plates and a single inconspicuous hinge. Gives off musky odor.

Similar Species Mud turtles (*Kinosternon* species), 3–6½", have large lower shells with 2 hinges; south-central and SE. United States.

Habitat Quiet or slow-moving waters with mud bottom; permanent ponds, clear lakes, rivers, and backwater sloughs.

Range S. Wisconsin, S. Ontario, and coastal Maine south to Florida and central Texas.

Loggerhead *Caretta caretta*

Seven sea turtle species visit our waters. These include the seven-foot-long Leatherback (*Dermochelys coriacea*), the largest living turtle, and the endangered Kemp's Ridley, the smallest sea turtle. The Loggerhead is most often encountered along the Atlantic and Gulf coasts in summer, where it nests from Texas to Virginia. Many of these ocean dwellers perish: Hatchlings confused by highway lights are drawn toward them instead of the sea; adults drown in fishing nets.

Identification 31–48″. Huge, with reddish-brown, heart-shaped upper shell and paddlelike flippers; head massive. Hatchlings have 3 keels on back and 2 on belly.

Similar Species Green turtles (*Chelonia* species), 28–60″, have single pair of elongated scales between eyes; warm seas. Kemp's Ridley (*Lepidochelys kempi*), 24–30″, has upper shell gray, almost circular; Gulf of Mexico to New England.

Habitat Coastal waters, bays, lagoons, and estuaries.

Range Tropical and subtropical seas; north to New England and S. California.

52

Common Snapping Turtle *Chelydra serpentina*

Although inoffensive underwater, snappers strike viciously when lifted from their habitat. Active day and night during warm months, they explore shallows for invertebrates, fish, carrion, and aquatic plants. In May and June, adults often move between bodies of water or travel overland to nesting sites, where females lay 25 to 50 round, white, flexible-shelled eggs in a flask-shaped cavity.

Identification   8–18½". Very large, brown or greenish, with massive head, powerful hooked jaws, and long tail sporting saw-toothed keels. Upper shell, often algae-covered, bears 3 low keels; lower shell cross-shaped. May exceed 50 lbs.

Similar Species   Alligator Snapping Turtle (*Macroclemys temmincki*) is largest freshwater turtle, 14–26", with 3 prominent keels on back; Mississippi Valley.

Habitat   Fresh and salt marshes, farm ponds, lakes, and creeks; prefers muddy-bottomed, weedy shallows.

Range   Rocky Mountains in Saskatchewan east through extreme S. Canada to Nova Scotia, south to Gulf of Mexico.

Wood Turtle *Clemmys insculpta*

During early spring, wood turtles are usually seen in water or basking nearby. Later they become more terrestrial; woodies are excellent climbers and may wander some distance in search of worms, slugs, berries, and succulent vegetation. In the fall, they return to an underwater retreat to hibernate. This species suffers from habitat loss and overcollecting.

Identification 5–9". Upper shell looks like a wooden sculpture; growth ridges pronounced. Lower shell yellow with black blotches, unhinged. Neck yellow to reddish-orange.

Similar Species Blanding's Turtle (*Emydoidea blandingi*): 6–10½", has bright yellow chin, hinged lower shell; Nebraska through Great Lakes region. Diamondback Terrapin has black-peppered gray neck.

Habitat Fast-moving woodland streams and nearby wet meadows; slow, soft-bottomed farmland streams.

Range E. Minnesota and NE. Iowa east through Great Lakes region and S. Quebec to Nova Scotia; south in the East to N. Virginia.

Diamondback Terrapin *Malaclemys terrapin*

Highly esteemed as a delicacy at the turn of the century, Diamondback Terrapins can still be found in New York City fish markets. Their numbers have been reduced by such market-hunting as well as by today's intensive coastal development. However, these turtles are still common in areas where their habitat remains intact, and can be seen basking on tidal flats. Females are twice as large as males and mature in about seven years—males earlier. Diamondbacks nest in June in the North, in April or May in southern regions.

Identification   4–9″. Gray head and neck peppered with black. Unusual sculptured shell; plates bear deep growth rings. Lower shell yellowish or greenish; not hinged. Eyes black and prominent; jaws light-colored.

Similar Species   Wood Turtle has yellow-orange neck.

Habitat   Coastal marshes, sheltered coves, and tidal channels bordered by cordgrass, lagoons behind barrier beaches, and brackish, mangrove-lined streams.

Range   Massachusetts to Texas along Atlantic and Gulf coasts.

Gopher Tortoise *Gopherus polyphemus*

Of the world's 250 turtles, about 40 species are tortoises. Adapted for arid habitats and a herbivorous diet, three of those known as gopher tortoises live in the United States: this species; the Texas Tortoise (*G. berlandieri*) of southern Texas; and the Desert Tortoise (*G. agassizii*) of southeastern California, southern Nevada, and western Arizona. The Gopher Tortoise digs burrows—temperature-stable shelters that are shared by many other animals. This ecologically important reptile is a protected species. Gopher Tortoises do not make good pets. Many thousands have been collected over the years, but few survive more than two or three months.

Identification	9–14½". Stout, with dome-shaped shell, elephantine hind legs, and shovel-like, heavily scaled front limbs.
Similar Species	Eastern Box Turtle has hinged lower shell.
Habitat	Sandhill country characterized by wire grass, turkey oak, and longleaf pine.
Range	Coastal Plain, extreme E. Louisiana east to S. South Carolina, south through Florida.

Pond Slider *Trachemys scripta*

This highly variable species includes the familiar Yellow-bellied Slider of the Southeast and the Red-eared Slider of the Mississippi Valley. Many millions have been hatched on turtle farms and sold as dime-store pets in countries around the world. A few have lived more than 30 years. These turtles are often seen stacked one upon another on a favorite basking log.

Identification 5–11½". Prominent yellow to red blotch or stripe behind eyes. Undersurface of chin appears rounded, not flat, when viewed head on, unlike related forms; V-shaped notch at front of upper jaw.

Similar Species Cooters (*Pseudemys concinna* and *P. floridana*), 6–16", have flattened lower jaw, upper jaw lacks V-shaped notch; SE. United States.

Habitat Sluggish streams and rivers, sloughs, swamps, ponds, and lake shallows; especially areas with lush vegetation.

Range Michigan and SE. Virginia south to New Mexico and N. Florida.

Eastern Box Turtle *Terrapene carolina*

Some box turtles are known to have survived more than 100 years. Surprisingly, these long-lived terrestrial vertebrates rarely venture more than a few acres during their lives. Box turtles are usually seen early in the day or after a rainstorm. During hot, dry periods, they may visit local wetlands or burrow into damp forest litter. They are fond of earthworms, slugs, raspberries, and mushrooms poisonous to people. Females lay three to eight eggs between May and June.

Identification 4–8½". High-domed upper shell variable in color and pattern; lower shell patternless or with dark blotching. Movable hinge allows lower shell to close tightly against upper. Males have red eyes and a concave lower shell; females have brown eyes.

Similar Species Western Box Turtle has ornately marked lower shell. Gopher Tortoise lacks hinged lower shell.

Habitat Moist woodlands and adjacent damp meadows, pastures, boggy fens, and floodplains.

Range Michigan to S. Maine south to E. Texas and Florida.

Western Box Turtle *Terrapene ornata*

In spring and fall, box turtles are active during the warm parts of the day, seeking grasshoppers, caterpillars, ground cherries, and pricklypear cactus. In cattle country, they methodically search dung piles for beetles. These turtles avoid midday summer sun by retreating under bushes or into burrows. They can often be seen moving about after a drenching downpour. The box turtles' ability to tightly seal their shell protects adults from almost all bird and mammal predators.

Identification   4–5¾". Ornately marked; high-domed upper shell bears distinctive pattern of radiating yellow lines, lower shell similarly patterned. Distinct hinge allows upper and lower shells to close tightly. Male has red eyes and female yellowish-brown eyes.

Similar Species   Eastern Box Turtle lacks ornate pattern on lower shell.

Habitat   Primarily dry prairies; also grazed pastures, dry open woodlands, and along waterways in arid terrain.

Range   S. South Dakota, S. Wisconsin, and NW. Indiana south into SE. Arizona, all of Texas, and SW. Louisiana.

Spotted Turtle *Clemmys guttata*

The Spotted is unquestionably one of our handsomest turtles. Although occasionally seen during winter warm spells, it usually leaves its winter retreat in March and is most visible from April to June, when it searches for aquatic invertebrates or basks on streamside tussocks. Dense vegetation hides its summer movements. It hibernates underwater in a communal den, often an abandoned muskrat burrow.

Identification 3½–5". Smooth black upper shell, head, and limbs sprinkled with round yellow spots.

Similar Species Bog Turtle (*C. muhlenbergii*), 3–4½", has upper shell unspotted, orange blotch behind eye; New York to Georgia. Blanding's Turtle has hinged lower shell.

Habitat Shallow, muddy-bottomed streams and adjacent wet meadows and pastures, beaver ponds, and red maple swamps. Enters brackish tidal creeks and salt marshes.

Range Michigan and N. Indiana east through S. Canada and Pennsylvania to Atlantic Coast; S. Maine south along Coastal Plain to N. Florida.

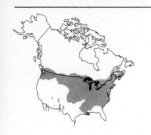

Painted Turtle *Chrysemys picta*

This is North America's most widespread turtle. In spring during early morning and afternoon scores can be seen sunning together on a favorite log. In between times, they re-enter the water to forage for tiny animals and aquatic plants. Basking raises the turtle's body temperature, activating its digestive enzymes.

Identification
4–10″. Low, oval upper shell smooth and unkeeled, olive-green to black; marginal plates accented by red bars or crescents. Lower shell light yellow to deep red, plain or intricately patterned. Yellow and red stripes on head and legs.

Similar Species
Chicken Turtle (*Deirochelys reticularia*), 5–10″, has long striped neck, and vertically striped rear legs; SE. Coastal Plain.

Habitat
Slow-moving streams and ponds; weedy shallows of rivers and lakes with muddy bottom and basking logs.

Range
British Columbia to Nova Scotia; south to Oregon, Wyoming, Oklahoma, Louisiana, and Georgia; scattered in Southwest.

Spiny Softshell *Trionyx spiniferus*

Softshells are easily spooked; if caught basking on a mudflat or sandbar, they return to water with startling speed. These adept aquatic predators are equipped with a long, flexible neck, low-profile shell, and broadly webbed feet that enable them to ambush and quickly overtake crayfish and small fish. They may lie buried in the mud, occasionally "snorkeling" to the surface with their nostrils. They are difficult to handle and will not hesitate to bite.

Identification   5–20". Pancakelike shell covered with soft, leathery skin. Spiny tubercles on leading edge of upper shell. Nostrils have lateral ridge.

Similar Species   Smooth Softshell (*T. muticus*), 5–14", has smooth upper shell, round nostrils; central United States.

Habitat   Primarily free-flowing streams and rivers with sandy or muddy bottom; also permanent ponds or large lakes.

Range   Throughout central and SE. United States in Mississippi River basin and other major river drainages; introduced to S. New Jersey, Arizona, and S. California.

72

△ **Cottonmouth** *Agkistrodon piscivorus*

When agitated, this snake is instantly recognizable by its bizarre defensive behavior—a gaping mouth. If you can see the "cotton" lining, you're too close! Bites are dangerous. Do not handle! Unlike harmless aquatic snakes, the pugnacious Water Moccasin—another name—is slow to retreat, and when it swims, it carries its head well out of water. Its varied diet includes frogs, fish, baby alligators, snakes, birds, and small mammals. Venomous.

Identification 20–74½". Heavy-bodied, with flat, lance-shaped head. Body patternless or with serrated crossbands. Young patterned; tail yellow-tipped. Scales keeled.

Similar Species Common Water Snake does not gape when alarmed; it and other harmless water snakes lack facial pit, have round pupils, and double row of scales beneath tail.

Habitat Swamplands, sloughs, irrigation ditches, and streams in pine flatwoods; oxbows in wooded river bottoms.

Range S. Missouri, S. Illinois, and SE. Virginia south to central Texas and Florida Keys.

74

⊖ **Copperhead** *Agkistrodon contortrix*

This is the most common poisonous snake in the East. During the summer Copperheads are nocturnal; they are found in rural areas under refuse, around dilapidated buildings and stone walls, or in sawdust heaps. These snakes eat mice, frogs, and cicadas. The young twitch their yellow-tipped tails to lure prey. Copperheads are not aggressive; their bites are painful but usually not life threatening. Venomous.

Identification
22–53″. Broad, coppery head distinctly wider than neck, with deep pit between eye and nostrils. Copper, orange, or pinkish body with bold chestnut crossbands, often hourglass- or dumbell-shaped and narrowest at midline of back. Scales keeled.

Similar Species
Milk and Corn snakes have narrow heads, lack deep pit between eyes and nostrils.

Habitat
Rocky, wooded hillsides near water, coastal flatwoods, swamp edges, and canyon springs.

Range
SE. Nebraska to SW. Massachusetts south to Trans-Pecos Texas and Florida panhandle.

76

△ **Massasauga** *Sistrurus catenatus*

Two pygmy rattlesnakes (*Sistrurus* species) are found north of Mexico. They differ from our other 13 rattlers (*Crotalus* species) by having nine large scales on the crown of the head, a characteristic they share with most nonpoisonous snakes. The Pygmy Rattler of southern pine flatwoods and wetlands is the least dangerous, but the larger Massasauga has highly toxic venom; luckily, it is timid; bites are rare and venom yield low. Its rattle produces a grasshopperlike buzzing. Venomous.

Identification   18–39½″. Dark bars on crown, often lyre-shaped, extending onto neck. Tail and rattle well developed.

Similar Species   Pygmy Rattlesnake (*S. miliarius*), 15–31″, has prominent stripes on head, small delicate rattle on slender tail; SE. United States. Timber Rattlesnake lacks head markings.

Habitat   In the East, bogs, swamps, wet prairies, and river bottoms; in the West, dry prairies and desert grasslands.

Range   S. Ontario and central New York southwest to SE. Arizona and Gulf Coast of Texas.

◬ **Eastern Diamondback Rattlesnake** *Crotalus adamanteus*

Our largest rattler, this is the most dangerous snake in the United States. Its bites can be life threatening, so give it a wide berth. The Diamondback resides in stump holes, Gopher Tortoise burrows, and brush piles. Its prey includes rabbits, squirrels, and cotton rats. Populations of this valuable rodent-predator have declined at an alarming rate as a result of rapid suburban development and commercial rattlesnake roundups. Venomous.

Identification
36–96″. Big, heavy-bodied, with dark, diamond-shaped blotches sharply outlined with a row of cream-colored scales. Two prominent, light, diagonal lines on side of face.

Similar Species
Canebrake, the southern Timber Rattlesnake, lacks prominent diamondlike body blotches.

Habitat
Pine flatwoods, dry, longleaf pine-turkey oak sandhills, palmetto thickets, and abandoned farmlands.

Range
Lower Coastal Plain, S. Mississippi eastward to SE. North Carolina, south to Florida Keys.

⊙ **Timber Rattlesnake** *Crotalus horridus*

Northern naturalists call this snake the Timber and southern woodsmen, the Canebrake. Its bad reputation is ill-deserved, for it is mild-mannered and often remains quietly coiled when approached, but its bite can be lethal. Active May to October; large numbers congregate in autumn in a den that has been used for generations. Venomous.

Identification 35–74½". Big, thick-bodied with black tail. Northern populations have 2 color phases, yellow and black. Dark brown blotches on back and sides of front third of body fuse into crossbands at midbody. Top of head yellow or black, unmarked. Southern populations have brown stripe through chevronlike crossbands.

Similar Species Massasauga has prominent markings on head.

Habitat In the North, remote rocky hillsides; in the South, wet pine flatwoods, river bottoms, and canebrakes.

Range SE. Minnesota to S. New Hampshire, south to E. Texas and N. Florida.

82

⬡ **Western Rattlesnake** *Crotalus viridis*

Our widest-ranging western rattlesnake, this species is highly variable in size, color, and temperament; nine races have been described. The one shown, found from Iowa to the Rockies, enjoys the largest distribution. It is easily excited and may become aggressive if disturbed. Active April to October, large numbers may hibernate together at a common den in winter. Venomous.

Identification 16–64". Brownish oval, hexagonal, or square blotches down center of back narrow to crossbands near tail. Light stripe behind eye, extending above corner of mouth.

Similar Species Mojave Rattlesnake has black-and-white ringed tail.

Habitat Pacific Coast sand dunes and coniferous northwestern forests to timberline in the Rockies, and into Great Plains grasslands and southwestern desert scrub.

Range W. United States and adjacent S. Canada.

⬿ **Mojave Rattlesnake** *Crotalus scutulatus*

Often confused with the Western Diamondback, the Mojave Rattlesnake isn't very excitable and is much less likely to display the classic S-loop striking coil. Yet, it is one of the most dangerous snakes in North America. Its venom contains a powerful toxin that attacks the respiratory system. Most rattler bites occur within a mile of home; the majority of victims are young men. Venomous.

Identification 24–51″. Tail encircled by wide white and narrow black tail rings. Well defined light-edged brown diamonds mark midline of back.

Similar Species Western Diamondback Rattlesnake (*C. atrox*), 34–84″, the biggest rattler in the West, has white and black tail rings of nearly equal width; SW. United States. Western Rattlesnake lacks black and white tail rings.

Habitat Open, flat, or rolling desert in arid grasslands.

Range SE. California and S. Nevada southeastward through Arizona and SW. New Mexico into the Big Bend region of Texas and Mexico.

86

Bullsnake *Pituophis melanoleucus*

The impressively powerful Bullsnake puts on quite a show when cornered—it swells up, hisses loudly, vibrates its tail, and lunges at its aggressor. But the bluff stops there: It bites! Called Pine Snakes east of the Mississippi, Bullsnakes take refuge in mammal or tortoise burrows and often overwinter with Racers, Rat Snakes, and rattlesnakes. These snakes are cited as the farmer's friend, as they consume large numbers of pesky mice, rats, and pocket gophers.

Identification	48–100″. Large constrictor. Head relatively small; large triangular scale covers snout. Often light-colored, with black, brown, or reddish-brown blotches on back and sides. Scales keeled.
Similar Species	Common Kingsnake and Rat Snake lack enlarged scale on snout.
Habitat	Dry, open pinewoods, sandhills, prairies, brushlands, desert, chaparral, farmlands; sea level to 9,000′.
Range	Pacific to Atlantic Coast; SW. Canada, Minnesota, Wisconsin, S. New Jersey, south to Guatemala.

88

Eastern Hognose Snake *Heterodon platyrhinos*

Because of its extraordinary defense exhibition, the Hognose is often called Puff Adder or Spreading Viper. When threatened, it hoods its neck, inflates its body, hisses loudly, then strikes. This actor, however, is harmless and doesn't bite. If further provoked, the snake rolls over, gapes its mouth, and plays dead. A burrower, it is specialized for eating toads.

Identification 20–45½″. Stout body. Upturned snout and wide neck. Color patterns extremely variable; usually with squarish dark blotches interspaced with light blotches; some all-black. Underside of tail lighter than belly.

Similar Species Western Hognose (*H. nasicus*), 16–35″, has black blotches on underside of tail; E. Montana and SE. Arizona eastward to central Illinois.

Habitat Prefers sandy or loamy soils; beaches, open fields, pine barrens, wooded hillsides, and wet prairies.

Range SE. South Dakota and central Minnesota to S. New England, south through central Texas and Florida.

Milk Snake *Lampropeltis triangulum*

Found from Canada to Ecuador, the Milk Snake has one of the largest ranges of any snake; more than 20 races have been described. In the North it is mistaken for the Copperhead, and in the South, for the Coral Snake. It is a secretive mouser often seen amid rotting logs, boards, or under surface litter.

Identification   14–78¼". Slender. Usually tricolored: ringed and blotched with red or brown, black, and yellow or white. Light neck collar followed by black-bordered red bands separated by light rings, which widen near belly. Northeastern form: V- or Y-shaped patch on neck and black-bordered brown to reddish saddles on back. Scales smooth.

Similar Species   Eastern Coral Snake has black nose. Corn Snake has keeled scales. Copperhead has unmarked head.

Habitat   Coastal woodlands through eastern uplands, and prairies to Rockies and tropical forests; sea level to 9,000'.

Range   Montana and Utah to Atlantic Coast.

92

Corn Snake *Elaphe guttata*

The beautiful Corn Snake is often seen around farm buildings, trash piles, and other places where mice thrive. It spends the day in stump holes or animal burrows, leaving its retreat in early evening to prowl for food. Although mostly found on the ground, the Corn Snake is an excellent climber.

Identification
24–72″. Eastern race, called the Red Rat Snake, is reddish-orange, gray, or brown, with prominent reddish blotches outlined in black. Western race, Great Plains Rat Snake, has grayish back with brownish blotches. Both have spear-pointed mark on head, checkered belly, and stripes under tail. Scales weakly keeled.

Similar Species
Milk Snake and Prairie Kingsnake have smooth scales. Immature Rat Snake lacks spear-point mark.

Habitat
Pine flatwoods, sandhills, rocky hillsides, woodland edges, and near streamlets and springs in the West.

Range
SE. Colorado to S. New Jersey, south through E. New Mexico, Texas, and Florida Keys; isolated population E. Utah to W. Colorado.

Prairie Kingsnake *Lampropeltis calligaster*

These constrictors are accomplished burrowers and are quite secretive in their surface movements. They search for small mammals and reptiles under leaves, logs, and other surface litter during the day but are most apt to be seen crossing roads on warm spring or summer nights. When first approached, Prairie Kingsnakes vibrate their tails rapidly and often hiss and strike to intimidate their adversaries.

Identification 30–52". Basic color may vary from tan to grayish-brown or yellowish-brown. Black-edged brown blotches on back; 2 alternating rows of smaller spots on sides. V-shaped arrowhead mark on crown. Markings on older animals may be obscure. Scales smooth.

Similar Species Corn Snake has keeled scales and stripes under tail. Rat Snake has keeled scales.

Habitat Pine flatwoods, open upland hardwood forests, rocky wooded hillsides, prairies.

Range SE. Nebraska and central Maryland to E. Texas and N. Florida.

Common Water Snake *Nerodia sipedon*

Often mistaken for the dreaded Cottonmouth of the South, many nonvenomous water snakes like this one are senselessly killed on sight. They can be seen basking on rocks or snags, especially along impoundment dikes and causeways; when frightened, they dive into the water and hide under submerged rocks or brush. If grabbed, they savagely bite the aggressor. Contrary to popular belief, these snakes do not deplete fisheries.

Identification 22–53″. Large, rough-scaled. Dark crossbands on neck and alternating dark blotches on back and sides at midbody. Belly with dark crescent-shaped spots. Scales in 21–25 rows.

Similar Species Southern Water Snake (*N. fasciata*), 16–62½″; dark stripe from eye to angle of mouth; Coastal Plain, North Carolina to E. Texas; lower Mississippi Valley.

Habitat Wetlands with sunny exposures; marshes, ponds, lakes, drainage ditches, and streams.

Range E. Colorado through E. United States and S. Canada except SE. Coastal Plain.

⬨ **Eastern Coral Snake** *Micrurus fulvius*

Do not handle! All coral snakes, large and small, bite and are deadly. Don't confuse this snake with its harmless mimics, the Scarlet Snake and the Scarlet Kingsnake. Coral snakes move about under surface litter in search of small lizards and snakes. The Western Coral Snake (*Micruroides euryxanthus*) is found in central Arizona and southwestern New Mexico. Venomous.

Identification	22–47½". Snout tip black, blunt. Broad yellow band across back of head. Wide black and red body bands separated by narrow yellow rings.
Similar Species	Scarlet Snake (*Cemophora coccinea*), 14–32", has pointed red snout, glossy white belly. Scarlet Kingsnake, southeastern form of Milk Snake, has somewhat pointed red snout, and bands circle body. Both SE. United States.
Habitat	Pine flatwoods, sandhill country, moist hammocks; cedar brakes and rocky hillsides in central Texas.
Range	S. Texas eastward along Coastal Plain to SE. North Carolina, south into Florida Keys.

Common Kingsnake *Lampropeltis getulus*

Kingsnakes are often seen around dilapidated wooden buildings, abandoned farms, old sawdust piles, and rural trash heaps. They are usually active by day but during midsummer become active at night. Unfortunately, these terrestrial snakes are rather slow moving and thus are easily killed or captured. When first handled they expel musk and try to bite, but tame quickly. Kingsnakes are constrictors, preying on snakes, rodents, and birds.

Identification   36–82″. Large, glossy, and smooth-scaled; chocolate-brown to black, with highly variable pattern. Light-centered scales may form chain links, crossbands, blotches, or speckles on back.

Similar Species   Rat Snake has weakly keeled rows. Racer has 17 scale rows.

Habitat   New Jersey Pine Barrens to Florida Everglades; southern pinelands and swamps, central rocky wooded hillsides, prairies, and western deserts and chaparral.

Range   SW. Oregon, Nebraska, and S. New Jersey, south to Baja California, Gulf of Mexico, and S. Florida.

102

Ringneck Snake *Diadophis punctatus*

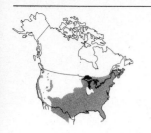

Although secretive, this docile snake is often encountered by exploring children. When found, it hides its head and curls its tail upside down to expose the brightly colored underside. If seized, it thrashes about and discharges a foul-smelling musk. The Ringneck eats earthworms, salamanders, and tiny snakes.

Identification 10–30″. Conspicuous yellow, cream, or orange neck ring. Bright yellow to red belly, often marked with black spots. Scales smooth.

Similar Species Brown Snake has keeled scales. Plains Black-headed Snake lacks black spots on belly.

Habitat Moist places beneath flat rocks, inside rotting logs, under leaf litter in cool forests, dry prairie hillsides, chaparral, and into deserts along streams.

Range Pacific to Atlantic Coast. S. Washington to Baja California and scattered in the West; Wisconsin to Nova Scotia south to Arizona and Florida Keys.

Rat Snake *Elaphe obsoleta*

Excellent climbers, Rat Snakes often reside in tree hollows well above the ground. These constrictors search the rafters of old farm buildings for mice and nesting birds. Rat Snakes often share winter dens with rattlesnakes and Copperheads; hence, the local names Rattlesnake Pilot and Pilot Black Snake.

Identification 34–101″. Three basic adult color patterns: plain black with white showing between scales (North); 4 dark stripes on yellow, orange, brown, or gray background (Atlantic Coastal Plain); dark blotches on gray, yellow, or brown back (Mississippi Valley and Gulf Coastal Plain). All young vividly blotched. Belly scales flat, with ends angled up sharply. Scales weakly keeled; usually 25–27 rows.

Similar Species Racer has smooth scales and rounded belly.

Habitat Hardwood forests, rocky wooded hillsides, rivers, swamps, live oak hammocks, farmlands, barnyards.

Range SE. Minnesota to SW. New England, south to Texas and Florida Keys.

106

Racer *Coluber constrictor*

The Racer, like the Coachwhip, is an alert, active daytime sight hunter. It is often seen streaking across roads. Contrary to popular belief, the Racer does not chase humans. If cornered, it may vibrate its tail against dry vegetation, which makes it sound convincingly like a rattler. Racers lay their eggs in rotted logs, sawdust piles, or under stones.

Identification 34–77″. Slender, uniformly colored; adults black, blue, brown, or greenish on back, with dark gray, white, or yellow belly. Young have reddish-brown saddles on back. Scales smooth, in 17 rows.

Similar Species Indigo Snake (*Drymarchon corais*), 60–103½″, our largest snake, is stout and blue-black, its throat suffused with cream, rust, or red; SE. Georgia, Florida, S. Texas. Rat Snake has flat belly scales.

Habitat Dry and moist environments; brushy dunes and hillsides, forest edges, stream and lake margins, prairies, sagebrush flats, chaparral, old farmlands.

Range Pacific to Atlantic Coast; some isolated in Southwest.

108

Rough Green Snake *Opheodrys aestivus*

During the day this delicate tree-dweller moves gracefully along branches in search of spiders and insects. It is quite mild-mannered, rarely tries to bite, and largely depends upon camouflage for protection. It may take to water when threatened, however. In summer, it may lay 3 to 12 eggs at a choice site shared by a number of females.

Identification 22–45½". Slender, long-tailed. Uniformly grass-green; underside plain greenish-yellow. Scales keeled, in 17 rows.

Similar Species Smooth Green Snake (*O. vernalis*), 14–26", has smooth scales, in 15 rows; Saskatchewan to Nova Scotia, south in scattered populations to New Mexico, SE. Texas, and North Carolina.

Habitat Prefers tangles of vines and overhanging vegetation bordering lakes and streams.

Range E. Kansas to S. New Jersey south through Texas and Florida Keys.

Coachwhip *Masticophis flagellum*

Few snakes can match the Coachwhip's speed. It is extremely active and agile, prowling about in search of lizards, snakes, and small rodents with its head and neck raised well above the ground and chasing down startled prey. Coachwhips move in short spurts, stopping to survey their habitat. They are very difficult to catch and bite repeatedly when captured.

Identification | 36–102″. Slim-bodied; eastern form typically has dark brown to black head and neck, fading to light brown at midbody; western form yellow, tan, gray, or pinkish; patternless or crossbars on neck. Scales smooth.

Similar Species | Striped Whipsnake (*M. taeniatus*), 40–72″, has light lengthwise stripes on each side; south-central Washington through Great Basin to S. New Mexico and S. Texas.

Habitat | Dry, open areas; pine flatwoods, rocky hillsides, grassy dunes, prairies, desert scrub, chaparral.

Range | Central California to S. South Carolina.

112

Plains Black-headed Snake *Tantilla nigriceps*

Some 40 black-headed snakes have been described from the central United States to Argentina; 10 occur within the range of this guide. Although often common, they are infrequently seen because they are nocturnal and spend most of their lives under rocks, surface litter, or underground. They eat centipedes, millipedes, spiders, and insect larvae.

Identification 7–14¾". Scales smooth. Uniformly brown, with distinct black cap; cap often pointed at rear and does not reach corner of mouth. No light collar.

Similar Species Flat-headed Snake (*T. gracilis*), 7–9½", has very pale cap, concave at rear; south-central United States. Southeastern Crowned Snake (*T. coronata*), 5–13", has distinct black cap that extends to corner of mouth, broad light collar borders cap; SE. United States.

Habitat Rocky areas in desert scrub, grasslands, and dry woodlands.

Range SW. Nebraska south through SE. Arizona and central Texas into Mexico.

114

Brown Snake *Storeria dekayi*

Often called DeKay's Snake, after the early New York naturalist, this docile serpent is ubiquitous in its range. It is usually seen under surface litter or flat rocks and moves about on warm, rainy nights. Brown Snakes eat slugs and earthworms. About a dozen, three- to four-inch-long young are born in summer.

Identification 10–20 ¾". Gray, brown, or reddish-brown back with indistinct back stripe bordered by a double row of small dark spots; belly pale cream, tan, or pinkish. Scales strongly keeled, in 17 rows.

Similar Species Red-bellied Snake (*S. occipitomaculata*), 8–16", has red belly, 15 scale rows; Saskatchewan to Nova Scotia, south to E. Texas, central Florida. Common Garter Snake has a light stripe on each side of body.

Habitat Coastal marshlands to moist upland forests; trash heaps in vacant city lots and leaf piles in suburbs.

Range Widespread in E. United States; ranges into S. Ontario and S. Quebec.

116

Rosy Boa *Lichanura trivirgata*

As its name implies, the Rosy Boa is kin to the world's giant snakes—the tropical American Boa Constrictor and Anaconda—and more distantly to Old World pythons. The Rosy and the Rubber are the two boas native to the United States. Primarily nocturnal and terrestrial, the Rosy Boa is a constrictor and preys on small mammals and birds. It is usually docile; when disturbed, it may defensively coil into a tight ball with its head hidden.

Identification 24–44″. Smooth, shiny, and stout, with short blunt head and tail. Tiny eyes with vertical pupils. Three broad brown stripes down body.

Similar Species Rubber Boa (*Charina bottae*), 13–33″, is uniformly colored, resembling fake rubber snake; British Columbia to Montana, south to S. California and Utah.

Habitat Arid rocky scrub and brushlands and desert, particularly near streams and spring seeps.

Range S. California, SW. Arizona, and adjacent Mexico.

118

Common Garter Snake *Thamnophis sirtalis*

The well-known "garden snake" is amazingly cold tolerant, surviving farther north than any other North American reptile. It is harmless, but when seized, it doesn't hesitate to bite. The Common Garter Snake is an active daytime predator, seeking out earthworms, fish, amphibians, and small mammals. In summer, large females may deliver 50 or more young.

Identification 18–52″. Color and pattern highly variable, but 3 back and side stripes are usually well defined. Side stripe on 2nd and 3rd scale rows. Scales keeled, in 19 rows.

Similar Species Western Terrestrial Garter Snake (*T. elegans*), 18–43″, has enlarged 6th and 7th upper lip scales; W. United States. Plains Garter Snake (*T. radix*), 20–42″, has 21 scale rows, with side stripe on 3rd and 4th; Rockies through Great Plains to central Ohio.

Habitat Diverse situations, often near water, from sea level to elevations of 8,000′; meadows, woodland thickets, city parks, and suburban backyards.

Range Pacific to Atlantic Coast; absent from arid Southwest.

120

Eastern Ribbon Snake *Thamnophis sauritus*

Ribbon snakes are very alert and active, and are agile climbers. Though semi-aquatic, they are often encountered basking in shrubs; when disturbed, they quickly disappear into dense brush or take to water. Instead of diving as water snakes do, they glide gracefully across the surface. Ribbon snakes seldom bite when handled; they expel musk from glands at the base of the tail. They prey on small fish and frogs.

Identification 18–40″. Streamlined and long-tailed, with 3 bright, well-defined stripes; side stripe on 3rd and 4th scale rows. Light spot before eyes. Scales keeled, in 19 rows.

Similar Species Western Ribbon Snake (*T. proximus*), 19–48½″; resembles eastern form, but has pair of large, bright spots that touch atop head; central United States. Common Garter Snake is thicker, with side stripe on 2nd and 3rd scale rows.

Habitat Wet meadows, marshes, and weedy margins of meandering streams and lakes.

Range All states east of the Mississippi River.

122

Slender Glass Lizard *Ophisaurus attenuatus*

When handled, glass lizards thrash about vigorously, trying to escape. Often the tail shakes off or shatters into several pieces—hence the common name. Because they are legless, these lizards are frequently mistaken for snakes, but unlike snakes, they can blink their eyes. The scales are reinforced with bony plates, making their bodies feel stiff. Grooves along each side permit expansion of the body for ingesting food and laying eggs. This species eats invertebrates, small lizards, snakes, and newborn mice.

Identification
22–42". Legless; movable eyelids and external ear openings; groove along each side of body. Dark stripe runs down back; dark stripes or speckling present below groove along sides and under tail.

Similar Species
Eastern Glass Lizard (*O. ventralis*), 18–42", lacks stripes below groove and on back; SE. Coastal Plain.

Habitat
Dry grasslands, dry open woodlands, abandoned farms.

Range
SE. Nebraska to S. Wisconsin and east to E. Virginia, south through E. Texas and Florida.

Five-lined Skink *Eumeces fasciatus*

Three blue-tailed skinks commonly occur over much of the South. They are difficult to identify if not in hand. Although sometimes called "scorpions," these skinks are not venomous, so the folklore has no foundation. If caught, however, they will inflict a retaliatory nip. The Five-lined Skink likes to bask in shafts of sunlight on logs, fences, and rocks.

Identification 5–8″. Color varies with age: juveniles black, with 5 bright yellowish stripes and blue tail; striping may disappear in older skinks. Males all brown with reddish head. Scales smooth; middle row of scales on underside of tail enlarged.

Similar Species Broad-headed Skink is larger. Southeastern Five-lined Skink (*E. inexpectatus*), 5½–8½″, has scales all the same size on underside of tail.

Habitat Damp woodlands with abundant stumps, rotting logs, and rocky retreats; streambeds and suburban gardens.

Range E. Kansas, Great Lakes to New England, south to E. Texas and N. Florida.

126

Six-lined Racerunner *Cnemidophorus sexlineatus*

Of the 14 whiptail lizards that live in the United States, this is the only one to invade the East. Like its relatives, the Six-lined Racerunner is very fast, nervous, and constantly on the go, preying on insects and dashing from bush to bush, then circling them in short jerky movements. Because its optimum body temperature exceeds 100°F, this lizard is seen only on warm days. Racerunners are very difficult to catch and rely on speed for protection; they can run in 18-mph bursts as they zoom for cover.

Identification | 6–10½″. Streamlined, with whiplike tail; 6–7 light stripes on dark background without spotting. Back scales tiny and granular; belly scales rectangular. Male has bluish belly; young have bright blue tails.

Similar Species | Five-lined Skink has smooth, shiny, overlapping scales.

Habitat | Dry, open, well-drained places; prairies, road rights-of-way, grazing lands, sand dunes, woodland edges.

Range | S. South Dakota to Maryland, south to S. Texas and Florida Keys.

Green Anole *Anolis carolinensis*

Some 200 different anoles live in the American tropics. Only the Green Anole is native to the continental United States; four West Indian species have been introduced and are well established in Florida. Commonly called a chameleon, the Green Anole may be green or brown, depending on its body temperature, surroundings, or state of mind. It is very abundant in suburban areas around shrubbery or on window screens. At night its skin reflects a flashlight beam.

Identification   5–8". Slender; emerald-green, with pink throat fan. Can change color rapidly to mottled greens and browns to all brown; occasionally has light stripe on back.

Similar Species   Brown Anole (*A. sagrei*), 5–8⅜", is brown with a yellow to red-orange throat fan with white line; Florida.

Habitat   Diverse arboreal habitats: shrubs, vines, tall grasses, and palm fronds; also fences and walls of buildings.

Range   SE. Oklahoma east to coastal North Carolina and south through central Texas and Florida Keys.

Collared Lizard *Crotaphytus collaris*

Commonly called mountain boomer, the Collared Lizard is often spotted atop a favorite basking rock. It is difficult to approach. When frightened or in pursuit of grasshoppers or smaller lizards, it leaps from its sunning perch and runs on its hind legs like a miniature dinosaur. Look out: These creatures bite hard!

Identification 8–14″. Head big, tail long. Two prominent black collar bands. Color and pattern variable, but most have some greenish color. Scales smooth and granular.

Similar Species Crevice Spiny Lizard (*Sceloporus poinsetti*), 5–11½″, has a single black collar, dark crossbands on tail, and large spiny scales; S. Arizona into west-central Texas. Leopard Lizard (*Gambelia wislizenii*), 8–15″, lacks collar and has round dark brown spots; Great Basin into Baja California, and S. California to W. Texas.

Habitat Dry, sparsely vegetated rocky hillsides and associated gullies, canyons, and ledges.

Range SE. Utah to east-central Missouri, south through Arizona, and NW. Arkansas and Texas to Mexico.

Chuckwalla *Sauromalus obesus*

Chuckwallas are usually seen perched in a prominent spot on a rock along desert roads in late morning or afternoon. They bask until their bodies reach temperatures of about 100°F, whereupon they begin to look for food. These herbivorous lizards forage on creosote bush, mallow, indigo bush, sunflowers, and fruits. When frightened, Chuckwallas gulp air, inflate their bodies, and wedge themselves into a rock crevice.

Identification 11–16½". Large, potbellied, with loose folds of skin around neck and sides. Tail broad at base, blunt-tipped. Male usually has black head, chest, and forelegs; female tends to retain crossbands from youth.

Similar Species Desert Iguana (*Dipsosaurus dorsalis*), 10–16", has a relatively small head and a row of enlarged, keeled scales down center of back; S. Nevada, SE. California, and W. Arizona into Mexico.

Habitat Lava flows, rocky hillsides, and outcrops in creosote bush desert; sea level to 6,000'.

Range SE. California east to SW. Utah and W. Arizona.

134

Western Whiptail *Cnemidophorus tigris*

The Western Whiptail shares the West with a dozen other whiptails but it is one of the few that extends its range beyond the limits of the arid Southwest. Like its eastern relative, the Racerunner, it prowls its turf incessantly in search of insects. When disturbed, this speedster is gone in a flash.

Identification 8–12″. Slim-bodied, with long, whiplike tail. Back and sides may be spotted, barred, marbled, or checkered with black or dusky markings; 4–8 light or faded stripes may be present. Underside usually cream-colored, with black spots on throat and chest.

Similar Species Checkered Whiptail (*C. tesselatus*), 11–15½″, has rows of black bars or spots on back and enlarged scales in front of skin fold on neck; SE. Colorado, New Mexico, W. Texas.

Habitat Desert scrub and semi-arid, sparsely vegetated areas into open woodlands and pine forests in the mountains.

Range SE. Oregon and California east to S. Idaho, W. Colorado, S. New Mexico, and W. Texas.

136

Lesser Earless Lizard *Holbrookia maculatum*

Unlike snakes, most lizards have ear openings, but in the genus *Holbrookia* they are absent, perhaps as an adaptation to the species' habit of burrowing headfirst into sand. The Lesser shares this characteristic with the Greater Earless Lizard (*Cophosaurus texanus*), a somewhat larger species from Arizona, New Mexico, and Texas. Not particularly wary, it is easily caught.

Identification 4–5″. Small; lacks ear openings; complete fold of skin crosses throat. Underside of tail unmarked. Male has 2 blue-bordered black blotches on each side of belly.

Similar Species Side-blotched Lizard has ear openings. Zebra-tailed Lizard (*Callisaurus draconoides*), 6–9″, has ear openings. NW. Nevada through SE. California and SE. Arizona into Mexico.

Habitat Sandy or gravelly areas of western plains; washes, dry streambanks, farmlands; to 7,000′.

Range Extreme SE. Utah and south-central South Dakota south into Mexico and central Texas.

138

Side-blotched Lizard *Uta stansburiana*

The Side-blotched is one of the most abundant and frequently seen lizards in the dry regions of the West. Although terrestrial, it will climb on rocks to take advantage of the best basking spots. Bursts of feeding often follow basking; these voracious little lizards consume insects, scorpions, and spiders, but in turn, they fall prey to other lizards and birds. Consequently, they seldom venture far from burrows or crevices.

Identification 4–6¼″. Small, usually brownish, with dark blotch on each side of chest behind foreleg. Scales on back small, lacking spines. External ear openings; skin fold across throat.

Similar Species Lesser Earless Lizard has no external ear openings. Western Fence Lizard (*Sceloporus occidentalis*), 6–9¼″, is spiny, sides of belly blue; Pacific Coast to W. Utah, and Washington to Baja California.

Habitat Dry, sandy or gravelly areas with rocks and scattered vegetation; below sea level to 9,000′.

Range Central Washington south through S. California and W. Texas.

140

Eastern Fence Lizard *Sceloporus undulatus*

Collectively called spiny lizards because of the pointed scales on their backs, some 16 species of *Sceloporus* are found in the United States. The Eastern Fence Lizard is a confirmed basker. It is adept at evasive maneuvers, and will circle its perch and ascend higher to avoid capture.

Identification 3½–7½". Conspicuously keeled, spine-tipped scales. Gray to rusty brown, marked with chevrons, crossbars, or back stripes. Males have bluish patches on each side of belly and 2 widely separated blue patches on throat.

Similar Species Sagebrush Lizard (*S. graciosus*), 4–6¼", has rusty area behind front legs and black bar on shoulder; Pacific Coast to SW. South Dakota, and Washington to Baja California.

Habitat Dry, open woodlands, brush, prairies, sand dunes, open rocky hillsides, farmlands, and abandoned buildings.

Range Central Utah east to central New Jersey, south through Arizona to Mexico and to central Florida.

142

Texas Horned Lizard *Phrynosoma cornutum*

Commonly called the horny toad, this species is the best-known horned lizard in the United States. Although fierce-looking, it is timid and largely depends on camouflage to avoid detection. If captured, it may squirt blood from its eyelids. These lizards do not make good pets! They feed almost exclusively on large live ants and are adapted to high temperatures.

Identification 2½–7″. Head crowned with spines; center 2 are longest. Two rows of pointed scales fringe each side of belly. Dark lines radiate from eye.

Similar Species Short-horned Lizard (*P. douglassi*), 2½–5¾″, has crown of short stubby spines and single row of scales fringing belly; E. Washington and Oregon to W. Dakotas, south through Arizona and New Mexico into Mexico.

Habitat Dry, sparsely vegetated flatlands with some sandy or loamy soil for digging; sea level to 6,000′.

Range SE. Colorado and Kansas south to extreme SE. Arizona through Texas into NW. Louisiana.

144

⬡ **Gila Monster** *Heloderma suspectum*

The Gila Monster is the largest and only venomous lizard in the United States. The world's only other venomous lizard is the closely related Mexican Beaded Lizard (*H. horridum*). Both are found south of the border in Sonora. Gila Monsters have sharp-edged, grooved teeth that deliver venom instantaneously as the lizard bites down. Bites are extremely painful but rarely fatal. Though active by day, these animals spend more than 95 percent of their lives underground. They are seen on the surface in early morning or late afternoon, as well as on cloudy spring days. Gila Monsters are powerful diggers and good climbers. Venomous.

Identification | 16–22″. Head large, snout black-tipped; tail sausage-shaped. Scales beadlike; banded or reticulated color pattern of black and pink, orange, or yellow. Tongue black, forked.

Similar Species | Western Banded Gecko has soft skin and vertical pupils.

Habitat | Desert grass and scrublands into juniper-oak woodlands.

Range | S. Nevada through S. Arizona to SW. New Mexico.

146

Western Banded Gecko *Coleonyx variegatus*

Banded geckos are nocturnal and are usually seen crossing remote desert roads at night. Silhouetted by headlights against dark macadam, they are small, spindly, ghostlike critters. During the day they take refuge under rocks or surface litter. When frightened, a banded gecko runs with its tail curled over its back and emits a squeaking sound if caught. Another antipredator device is its break-away tail, which snaps off easily near the constriction at the base.

Identification 4½–6″. Eyes large, with protruding movable eyelids; pupils vertical. Soft, pliable skin; fine granular scales on back; 6–10 preanal pores in contact at midline.

Similar Species Texas Banded Gecko (*C. brevis*), 4–4¾″; 3–6 preanal pores with gap at midline; S. New Mexico to south-central Texas.

Habitat Desert grasslands, chaparral, and arid creosote and sagebrush country into pinyon-juniper woodlands.

Range S. California, S. Nevada, and SW. Utah southeast to extreme SW. New Mexico.

148

Great Plains Skink *Eumeces obsoletus*

This species is North America's largest skink. Like the Western Skink (*E. skiltonianus*), which ranges from British Columbia to Baja California and the Great Basin, it is active during the day but very secretive. Usually you will hear this skink in the underbrush before seeing it. Skinks often have regenerated tails, the result of earlier encounters with predators.

Identification 6½–13¾". Color varies from light tan to light brown; each scale edged in black. Scales on sides run diagonally to rows on back. Young black, with white spots on lip scales and blue tail.

Similar Species Gilbert's Skink (*E. gilberti*), 7–12¾", has side scales in parallel rows, more or less distinct light stripes on back; adults have red head and tail; central and S. California, S. Nevada, west-central Arizona.

Habitat Grasslands and woodlands, and in arid uplands along brush-bordered streams with rock outcrops.

Range S. Nebraska south to west-central Arizona, and through central Texas into Mexico.

150

Broad-headed Skink *Eumeces laticeps*

The largest eastern skink, the Broad-headed prefers warmer and drier situations than does the Five-lined Skink. This arboreal creature favors spreading live oaks and cypress trees as haunts. Females, depending on their size, lay 6 to 16 eggs from May to July in a tree cavity or under the bark of a dead tree. The mother attends the eggs until they hatch.

Identification 6½–12¾". Large, smooth-scaled; brown with 5 broad light stripes, which fade with age. Older males lose stripes and have a wide head, which is red during breeding season. Middle row of scales on underside of tail enlarged; 5 scales on upper lip before large scale below eye. Young black, with 5 stripes and blue tail; some have 7 stripes.

Similar Species Five-lined Skink has 4 upper lip scales.

Habitat Woodlands with large stumps and hollow trees, swamp-edged forests, vacant rubble-strewn urban lots.

Range SE. Kansas to SE. Pennsylvania, south through E. Texas and to central Florida.

152

Two-lined Salamander *Eurycea bislineata*

To find this salamander, look under objects at water's edge or in pockets of gravel in streamlets, where it feeds on aquatic insects. In winter or spring the female lays a flat cluster of eggs on the underside of a rock or log in running water, remaining with the eggs until the aquatic larvae hatch.

Identification 2½–4¾". Slender, with broad yellow or orange back stripe running from snout to tail tip; stripe flanked by dark line extending from eye well out onto tail. Five toes on hind foot.

Similar Species Dwarf Salamander (*E. quadridigitata*), 2–3½", is a miniature with 4 toes on hind foot; SE. Coastal Plain. Long-tailed Salamander (*E. longicauda*), 4–8", has a slender tail longer than its body, tail has vertical bars; S. New York southwest to N. Alabama and S. Illinois.

Habitat Rocky brooks, springs, and seepages in hardwood forests and swamplands; floodplains in Coastal Plain; to 6,000'.

Range SE. Ontario to mouth of St. Lawrence River, south to SE. Louisiana and Florida panhandle.

154

Northern Dusky Salamander *Desmognathus fuscus*

The abundant Northern Dusky is active at night on the surface and hides during the day under moist forest litter or rocks. When discovered, this elusive creature leaps into water to avoid capture. It is often found with the Red Salamander.

Identification 2½–5½". Pale line from eye to angle of jaw. Tail triangular, sharply keeled in cross section. Adults usually patterned with 6–7 pairs of oval or rhombic blotches, which often fuse into a back stripe.

Similar Species Mountain Dusky Salamander (*D. ochrophaeus*), 2¾–4½", has a rounded tail that ends in a filament; uplands, New York to NE. Georgia. Southern Dusky Salamander (*D. auriculatus*), 3–6½", is peppered with white or yellow on its belly; SE. Coastal Plain.

Habitat In the North, springs and rocky woodland creeks; in the South, swamps and clear or muddy streams and seepages in bottomland forests and ravines.

Range SE. Quebec and S. New Brunswick southwest to Louisiana and N. Georgia.

156

Tiger Salamander *Ambystoma tigrinum*

The world's largest land-dwelling salamander is a secretive subterranean dweller, living in animal burrows and rotted root tunnels. A heavy winter or spring rain may stimulate Tiger Salamanders to migrate to their breeding ponds. They are voracious predators of worms, large insects, and other amphibians.

Identification 6–13½". Chunky, with small eyes and wide, rounded snout. Tubercles on soles of feet. Color and pattern highly variable, often with light bars, spots, or blotches on a dark background. No parotoid glands.

Similar Species Marbled Salamander (*A. opacum*), 3½–5", has silvery crossbands and black belly; S. Illinois to S. New England, south to E. Texas and N. Florida.

Habitat Vicinity of ponds in moist mountain woodlands and pine savannas to prairies and arid sagebrush plains; sea level to 11,000'.

Range Widely distributed in the United States; absent from most of Great Basin, Mojave and Colorado deserts, the Appalachians, and S. Florida.

Spotted Salamander *Ambystoma maculatum*

A mole salamander, the Spotted dwells in secret underground retreats. Heavy rains and warming temperatures prompt its migration to breeding ponds, in March and April in northern areas and December to February in the South. This species often shares its breeding ponds with the fall-breeding Marbled Salamander (*A. opacum*). Spotties partake in an elaborate courtship ritual in which the female ultimately retrieves one of many sperm packets dropped by the male. Females lay one or more globular masses containing about 100 eggs.

Identification 6–9¾". Body robust; head black; 2 rows of round yellow or orange spots accent head and tail.

Similar Species Tiger Salamander's back markings are irregular in shape and distribution.

Habitat Boreal, upland, and lowland forests and woodlands with vernal pools and fishless ponds.

Range South-central Ontario to Nova Scotia, south to E. Texas and S. Georgia.

160

Slimy Salamander *Plethodon glutinosus*

This species is well named! Its skin glands secrete an innocuous gluey substance that is very difficult to remove from your fingers. As with other *Plethodon* species, the aquatic larval stage of growth is omitted. Slimys are nocturnal and are active spring through fall near the surface except during hot weather. A western look-alike, the Black Salamander (*Aneides flavipunctatus*) lives in northern California.

Identification 4½–8". Shiny black with small scattered white spots and brassy flecks atop head, back, and tail. Larger white, gray, or yellow spotting on sides.

Similar Species Wehrle's Salamander (*P. wehrlei*), 4¾–6¼", is much more slender, dark gray or brown; Appalachian plateau, SW. New York to NW. North Carolina.

Habitat Moist shale banks, shady ravine slopes, damp forested hillsides with rocky outcrops, and caves; to 5,000'.

Range S. New York south to central Florida and southwest to E. Oklahoma; scattered populations in S. New England and south-central Texas.

162

Red-backed Salamander *Plethodon cinereus*

Redbacks often occur in extraordinary abundance and are an extremely important part of the forest community's food base. Their counterpart in the coastal Pacific Northwest, the Western Redback (*P. vehiculum*), is the most numerous and wide-ranging western woodland salamander. Eggs are laid on land and larvae develop without an aquatic stage.

Identification	2½–5″. Body slender, often marked with broad, straight-edged stripe running down back from head to tail; stripe may be yellow, orange, or gray. A "lead-back" phase—light gray to black and unstriped—commonly occurs in some populations.
Similar Species	Zigzag Salamander (*P. dorsalis*), 2½–4¼″, has variably colored back stripe with wavy edges; central Indiana to central Alabama, and other isolated areas.
Habitat	Cool, damp hardwood, coniferous, and mixed forests.
Range	W. Ontario to Nova Scotia, south to S. Missouri and South Carolina.

164

Ensatina *Ensatina eschscholtzii*

Ensatinas come in an amazing array of colors and patterns—some are plain or finely speckled, others are boldly blotched, banded, or barred. They are frequently encountered under rotting woodland debris and rocks. Females brood their egg clutches in underground chambers. There is no aquatic larval stage. When threatened, the Ensatina assumes a stiff-legged, swaybacked stance with its tail positioned over its head; the tail easily snaps off if seized, allowing escape.

Identification 3–5¾". Tail swollen, constricted at base; 5 toes on hind foot. Base of limbs lighter than tip.

Similar Species Van Dyke Salamander (*Plethodon vandykei*), 3¾–4¾", lacks constriction at tail base; W. Washington.

Habitat Fir-maple forests in Northwest; redwood, oak-walnut, and pine-oak-cedar forests and chaparral to the south; to 10,000'.

Range SW. British Columbia to Baja California; absent from Central Valley, California.

166

Red Salamander *Pseudotriton ruber*

Look for this handsome creature near springs and cold brooks. Females nest in early fall and the aquatic larvae hatch in late fall or early winter, transforming in two and a half years. Males are mature at four years, females at five. Red Salamanders are color mimics of the highly toxic red eft, a land stage of the Eastern Newt, whose bright hue wards off predators.

Identification 3¾–7". Body chunky; red, peppered with many irregularly shaped black flecks. Eyes yellow.

Similar Species Mud Salamander (*P. montanus*), 3–7½", has well-separated round spots and brown eyes; chiefly Coastal Plain and Piedmont, S. New Jersey to central Florida; also S. Ohio to Tennessee. Spring Salamander (*Gyrinophilus porphyriticus*), 4½–8½", has light line from eye to nostril; S. Maine southwest to N. Alabama.

Habitat Cool, sheltered brooks, springs, seepages, and nearby damp woodlands and meadows; to 5,000'.

Range SE. Indiana to S. New York, south to SE. Louisiana and Florida panhandle.

168

Eastern Newt *Notophthalmus viridescens*

The Eastern Newt's life history differs markedly from that of a typical salamander. Between its aquatic stages as a larva with gills and as an adult without them—this newt lives on land for two or three years in a subadult, or eft, stage. Then it transforms into a sexually mature aquatic adult. Sometimes the eft stage is skipped; or, if ponds dry up, adults revert to efts. The eft is toxic; its bright color warns predators that it is inedible.

Identification 2½–5½". Aquatic adults olive-green, yellowish-green, or dark brown above; yellow below. Back and belly peppered with black dots. Efts are bright reddish-orange to reddish-brown. Skin rough; no grooves on sides.

Similar Species Red Salamander has smooth, slimy skin, grooves on sides.

Habitat Weedy lake shallows and ponds, backwaters of slow-moving streams, and swamps; efts in damp woodlands.

Range S. Ontario to Nova Scotia, south through E. Texas and Florida.

170

Rough-skinned Newt *Taricha granulosa*

Of the three Pacific newts, the Rough-skinned spends the most time in water. It is often seen wandering about on cool humid days. If disturbed, it strikes a bizarre defense swayback posture, with head and tail bent upward to expose the bright warning colors of its underside. Powerful toxins in its skin can kill most predators if ingested; garter snakes, an exception, can eat Rough-skinned Newts with impunity.

Identification 5–8½". Skin rough; no grooves on sides. Back dark brown to black, belly yellow to reddish-orange. Lower eyelids dark.

Similar Species Red-bellied Newt (*T. rivularis*), 5½–7½", has tomato-red belly and large, dark brown eyes; coastal California, north of San Francisco Bay. California Newt (*T. torosa*), 5–7¾", has light-colored lower eyelids; coastal California, W. Sierra Nevada slope.

Habitat Damp coastal forests and grasslands near ponds, lakes, and slow-moving streams; sea level to 9,000'.

Range Pacific Coast; SE. Alaska to west-central California.

172

Mudpuppy *Necturus maculosus*

This bizarre, primitive-looking aquatic salamander has been likened to the "missing link." It is most often seen by fishermen, who usually cut their lines rather than deal with the slimy creature. Active year-round, Mudpuppies may be drawn to the glow of lanterns in summer or worms or fish bait in winter. In spring, females attach about 100 eggs each to the underside of a rock, guarding them until they hatch.

Identification   8–17". Totally aquatic. Large, with feathery gills and compressed tail; 4 toes on feet.

Similar Species   Hellbender (*Cryptobranchus alleganiensis*), 12–29", the largest New World salamander, is also totally aquatic, and adults lack external gills; Susquehanna River drainage southwest to S. Illinois and NE. Mississippi; Black and White rivers in Missouri and Arkansas.

Habitat   From muddy, heavily vegetated river shallows to cold, clear, deep lakes.

Range   SE. Manitoba to S. Quebec, south to N. Louisiana and N. Georgia.

174

American Alligator *Alligator mississippiensis*

North America's largest reptile is a habitat engineer; during droughts, its " 'gator holes" provide water for other wildlife. Alligators demonstrate maternal care. In response to the calls of hatchlings, the female scratches open the nest and carries her young to water. These reptiles eat insects, fish, frogs, turtles, snakes, birds, and small mammals.

Identification 6–19'. Huge, gray-black, and heavily armored, with broad, rounded snout. Tail flattened from side to side. Large 4th tooth in bottom jaw fits into a socket in upper jaw; not visible when mouth is closed.

Similar Species American Crocodile (*Crocodylus acutus*), 7–15', has long, slender snout, 4th tooth exposed; Florida Bay. Spectacled Caiman (*Caiman crocodilus*), 4–8', has bony curved ridge between eyes; introduced S. Florida.

Habitat Fresh and brackish marshes, backwaters of large rivers, ponds, lakes, bayous, and big spring runs.

Range Coastal SE. North Carolina to Florida Keys, west to central Texas.

Guide to Orders and Families

Amphibians and reptiles belong to two different classes of vertebrates. Amphibians evolved from fishes some 350 million years ago and became the first vertebrates to live on land. Most amphibians are four-legged, have smooth, moist skin, and lay eggs with no shells in fresh water or in moist places on land.

Amphibians gave rise to reptiles about 300 million years ago. Unlike their ancestors, reptiles have dry skin covered with scales. Most reptiles lay eggs with a protective shell and a large yolk. The development of the shelled egg allowed reptiles to free themselves from water for reproduction and to become completely terrestrial.

These two classes—amphibians and reptiles—are further divided into orders and families. Knowing order and family characteristics will help you to identify species.

The Amphibians

Today's amphibians are divided into three major groups: salamanders (order Caudata), frogs and toads (order Salientia), and eel-like caecilians (order Gymnothiona). The first two orders occur in our range.

Salamanders

Unlike frogs and toads, the voiceless salamanders have slender bodies, long tails, distinct body regions, and front and hind legs of nearly equal size. They resemble lizards superficially, but lack the lizards' scaly skin, claws, and

178

external ears. Salamanders are secretive, nocturnal, and carnivorous.

Hellbender and The giant salamanders (family Cryptobranchidae) are
Mudpuppies strictly aquatic and include the largest living salamanders.
Only three species remain today, our two-foot Hellbender
and two species, which may exceed five feet in length, in
China and Japan. Like the Hellbender, the mudpuppies
(family Proteidae) are permanently aquatic, and retain gills
throughout life.

Newts and Other Unlike most salamanders, newts (family Salamandridae)
Salamanders have rough-textured skin. Eastern newts are primarily
aquatic, but the western species are terrestrial. The mole
salamanders (family Ambystomatidae), including the
Spotted and Tiger salamanders, live in underground
retreats and are rarely seen except during their short
breeding season. They are the largest terrestrial
salamanders. The lungless salamanders (family
Plethodontidae), such as the Northern Dusky or Red-
backed, are the most evolutionarily advanced salamanders.
All are lungless and breathe through their moist skin.

Frogs and Toads Found on every continent except Antarctica, frogs and
toads have colonized nearly all habitats except the hottest

179

deserts and coldest polar regions. Frogs and toads are known for their well-developed jumping legs. They lack tails as adults. Unlike salamanders, these amphibians have a well-developed ear and a voice to attract mates. Most species breed in water; eggs hatch into tadpoles which gradually metamorphose into young frogs.

True Frogs and Treefrogs All of the true frogs (family Ranidae) in the United States belong to the genus *Rana*, which includes the familiar Bull, Green, and Wood frogs. These are the large, slim-waisted, and long-legged frogs that typically live along the edge of water and are excellent jumpers. Treefrogs (family Hylidae) are well adapted to arboreal life. They are slim-bodied and have long, slender legs with sticky, adhesive toe pads used to walk along branches and climb trunks.

Toads and Spadefoots The familiar toads (family Bufonidae) are all short-legged, squat, and pot-bellied, with rough, warty skin. Large parotoid glands behind a toad's head secrete a white substance that irritates the mouth of would-be predators. Though they superficially resemble the true toads, our spadefoots (family Pelobatidae) can be identifed by their smooth skin, vertical pupils, and a dark, horny, sharp-edged "spade" on the inner surface of each hind foot.

180

The Reptiles   During the Age of Reptiles, there were 16 different reptilian orders. Only four remain today: turtles (order Chelonia), crocodilians (order Crocodylia), the lizardlike Tuatara from New Zealand (order Rhynchocephalia), and lizards and snakes (order Squamata).

Turtles   The first turtles appeared about 200 million years ago, considerably before the dinosaurs. Large land-dwelling turtles are often called tortoises, while those that are hard-shelled, edible, and aquatic are called terrapins. Structurally, turtles are truly bizarre, with expanded ribs incorporated into a protective shell, a unique placement of limb girdles inside the rib cage, and a horny beak instead of teeth. Turtles are not closely related to any other reptiles. Without exception, turtles lay eggs.

Freshwater Turtles and Tortoises   The snapping turtles (family Chelydridae) are the largest and most aggressive freshwater turtles, but are often confused with the mud and musk turtles (family Kinosternidae), which are smaller, oval-shaped, and have a hinged lower shell. The pond and river turtles (family Emydidae) are the largest turtle family, and include the familiar Painted, Spotted, and box turtles. They have plate-covered upper and lower shells and most are semi-

181

aquatic and omnivorous. The tortoises (family Testudinidae) are plant-eaters adapted to arid climates. The highly aquatic soft-shelled turtles (family Trionychidae) have a soft, leathery skin instead of plates over their nearly circular, pancakelike shells.

Marine Turtles   There are two families of marine turtles: the sea turtles (family Chelonidae) which include the Loggerhead, and the seven-foot Leatherback (family Dermochelyidae), the largest living turtle. The largest members of their order, marine turtles are found in warm-temperate and tropical waters.

Crocodilians   Alligators (family Alligatoridae) and crocodiles (family Crocodylidae) have changed little in the last 65 million years. These reptiles are large, with well-armored skin, sculptured heads, and protruding eyes and nostrils. All species are aquatic, fond of basking, and carnivorous.

Lizards   By far the most diversified group of reptiles, lizards show a bewildering array of sizes, shapes, and colors. Some lizards have tiny granular scales, but others are protected with relatively large and platelike, shinglelike, or beadlike scales. Most lizards are active during the day, eat invertebrates, and lay eggs.

Iguanas, Geckos, and Skinks

The iguanas (family Iguanidae) are the best known lizards in the New World; over 50 species are found in the United States. Some live in trees while others are terrestrial. Iguanas feed on insects and other invertebrates, but some eat vegetation. The geckos (family Gekkonidae) are notable for their ability to vocalize at night. Special structures on the bottom of their toe pads allow them to grip the slightest irregularities and to scale smooth walls and ceilings. The skinks (family Scincidae) have a sleek covering of polished, overlapping scales containing bony plates. Both geckos and skinks have a tail that breaks off very easily. This is an adaptation for escaping from predators.

Whiptails, Glass Lizards, and Gila Monsters

Our whiptails (family Teiidae) are the speedsters of the lizard world. Slender, with long whiplike tails and well-developed legs, they scurry about with rapid, jerky movements. The glass lizards (family Anguidae) of the Southeast are recognized by their elongated, shiny, and stiff bodies and delicate tails that break off easily. The gila monster family (family Helodermatidae) has two North American species. They are the only venomous lizards in the world and have stout tails and bodies, broad heads, and beadlike scales.

Snakes Despite the loss of legs, external ears, and eyelids, snakes are an amazingly successful group: About 2,400 species are known, and 115 live in North America. Most are terrestrial, but many are aquatic, marine, burrowers, or tree-dwellers. All snakes are carnivorous and swallow their prey whole. They continue to grow in length throughout their lives (some may live 40 years), but growth slows at maturity. Snakes periodically shed their outer layer of skin, often in one piece, beginning at the tip of their snout. Nineteen North American species are venomous; learn to recognize them quickly and leave them alone! Four families of snakes are covered in this book.

Boas and Colubrids The boas and pythons (family Boidae) include the giants of the snake world, but the relatively small Rubber and Rosy boas are our only representatives. The largest of all snake families is the colubrids (family Colubridae), a group of harmless snakes including such species as the Corn Snake, Rat Snake, and the Racer. They display a great range of physical characteristics. In general, the colubrid's head is wider than its neck and is topped with large, regularly arranged scales. The eyes are well developed, with round or vertical pupils. Belly scales are as wide as the body and those under the tail are typically divided. Colubrid habitats are as varied as their anatomy—from subterranean holes to treetops.

Pit Vipers and Coral Snakes Nearly all of the venomous snakes in the United States are pit vipers (family Viperidae). Their heads are triangular, distinctly wider than their necks, and have recurved, retractable, hollow fangs. A heat-sensitive pit, used to locate small mammals and birds, is present on each side of the head between the eye and nostril. Pit vipers have vertical pupils and an undivided row of scales under their tails. Most are nocturnal and bear their young alive. Our two coral snakes (family Elapidae) are related to the highly venomous cobras, kraits, mambas, and taipans. Unlike the pit vipers, their hollow fangs cannot be folded back.

Index

Numbers in italics refer to reptiles and amphibians mentioned as similar species.

187

The Audubon Society

The National Audubon Society is among the oldest and largest private conservation organizations in the world. With over 560,000 members and more than 500 local chapters across the country, the Society works in behalf of our natural heritage through environmental education and conservation action. It protects wildlife in more than seventy sanctuaries from coast to coast. It also operates outdoor education centers and ecology workshops and publishes the prizewinning AUDUBON magazine, AMERICAN BIRDS magazine, newsletters, films, and other educational materials. For further information regarding membership in the Society, write to the National Audubon Society, 950 Third Avenue, New York, New York 10022.